Independence Day

Piper Nelid

Rosen REAL READERS

Rosen Classroom™
New York

Today is Independence Day!
Independence Day is
a fun holiday.
It is celebrated every year.

It is also called
the Fourth of July.
This is an important day
in American history.

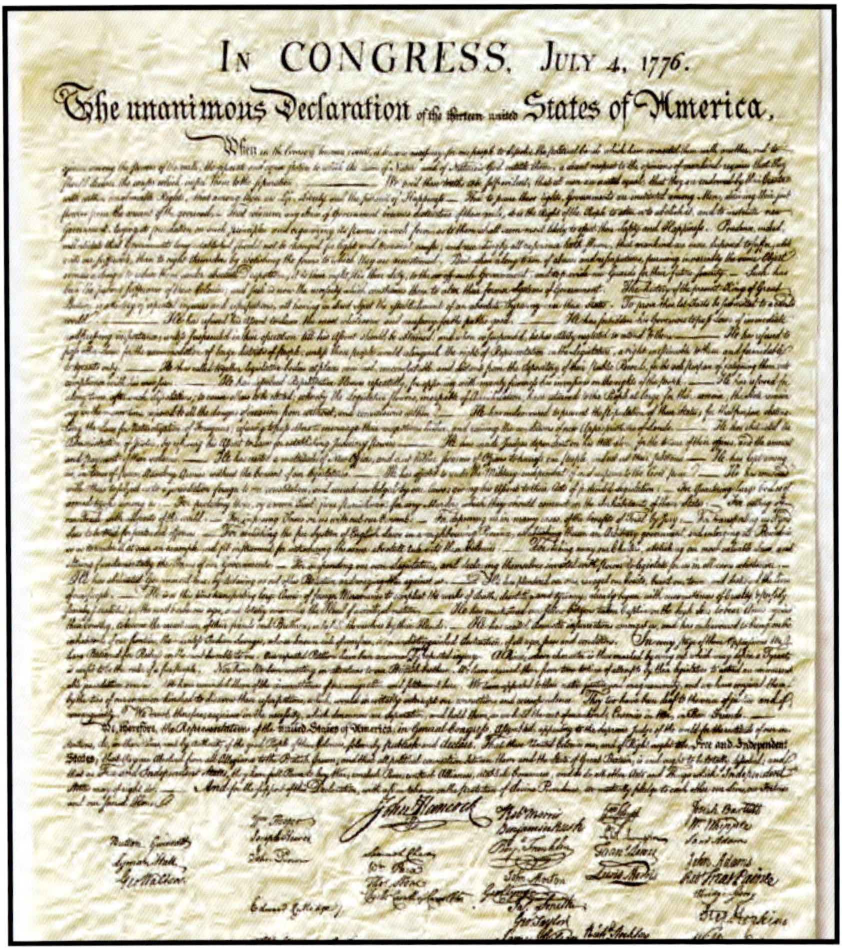
IN CONGRESS, JULY 4, 1776.

The unanimous Declaration of the thirteen united States of America,

The Declaration of Independence
was signed on July 4.
It was signed in 1776.
This is when America
was born.

This document was signed in
Philadelphia, Pennsylvania.
It was signed by
the Founding Fathers.

Independence Day is
the birthday of America.
Each year it is older.

I celebrate Independence Day
with my family.
We have a barbecue.
My dad cooks some food.

Some cities have contests.
My favorite is the
hot dog eating contest.

Other cities have parades.
I like seeing the marching band.

I like watching fireworks at night.
They are colorful and bright!

Independence Day is one of my favorite holidays.

Let's celebrate it together!

Words to Know

barbecue

birthday

contest

fireworks

Founding Fathers

parade